Dear Teacher:

The unique **STEP INTO READING**® series offers books at five carefully developed skill levels, tailor-made for the emergent reader. Promoting fluency and providing quality content, Step into Reading hits curricular topics and is perfect for integrating science, social studies, and even math. Step into Reading offers fiction and nonfiction favorites, and includes popular characters such as the Disney Princesses and Arthur who will excite even your most reluctant readers.

The exclusive **STEP INTO READING**® Teachers Edition you have in your hands includes five complete Step into Reading books, one for each step, to show you the value of this program for your classroom. For each step you will also find an innovative teachers guide, with common core standard correlations, and a book list. Enjoy!

Learning to Read, Step by Step!

Ready to Read   **Preschool–Kindergarten**
• Big Type and Easy Words • Rhyme and Rhythm • Picture Clues
For children who know the alphabet and are eager to begin reading. 32 pages

Reading with Help   **Preschool–Grade 1**
• Basic Vocabulary • Short Sentences • Simple Stories
For children who recognize familiar words and sound out new words with help. 32 pages

Reading on Your Own   **Grades 1–3**
• Engaging Characters • Easy-to-Follow Plots • Popular Topics
For children who are ready to read on their own. 48 pages

Reading Paragraphs   **Grades 2–3**
• Challenging Vocabulary • Short Paragraphs • Exciting Fiction and Nonfiction
For children who are reading simple sentences with confidence. 48 pages

Ready for Chapters   **Grades 2–4**
• Chapters • Longer Paragraphs • Fascinating Nonfiction
For children who want to take the plunge into chapter books, but still like colorful pictures. 48 pages

STEP INTO READING® is perfect for guided reading or any reading program!

For Charlie and Allison—D.M.R.
For Dad and Sherry—M.I.

With grateful acknowledgment to Frank Lange for his time and expertise in reviewing this book.

Text copyright © 2009 by Dana Meachen Rau
Illustrations copyright © 2009 by Melissa Iwai

Published in the United States by Random House Children's Books,
a division of Random House, Inc., New York.

Step into Reading, Random House, and the Random House colophon are
registered trademarks of Random House, Inc.

Visit us on the Web!
www.stepintoreading.com

Educators and librarians, for a variety of teaching tools, visit us at
www.randomhouse.com/teachers

Library of Congress Cataloging-in-Publication Data
Rau, Dana Meachen.
Corn aplenty / by Dana Meachen Rau ; illustrated by Melissa Iwai. — 1st ed.
  p.   cm. — (Step into reading. A step 1 book)
Summary: Two children watch a local farmer grow a crop of corn and as the corn
develops—from seed to harvest time—so does the friendship between the children and
the farmer.
ISBN 978-0-375-85575-7 (pbk.) — ISBN 978-0-375-95575-4 (lib. bdg.)
[1. Farmers—Fiction. 2. Corn—Fiction. 3. Friendship—Fiction.] I. Iwai, Melissa, ill. II. Title.
PZ7.R193975Co 2009
[E]—dc22   2008009716

Manufactured in China

10 9 8 7 6 5 4 3 2 1

First Edition

STEP INTO READING®

Corn Aplenty

by Dana Meachen Rau
illustrated by Melissa Iwai

Random House 🏠 New York

We drive by a farm.

The farmer

plows the field.

The dirt is
brown and bumpy.

We ride by the farm.

The farmer
plants the seeds.

The seeds are
yellow and small.

We skip by the farm.

The farmer
feeds the plants.

The seedlings are
green and soft.

We stop by the farm.

The farmer
waters the plants.

The stalks are
strong and tall.

We race to the farm.

The farmer
picks the corn.

The bins are
full and heavy.

We walk
to the farm stand.

The farmer
sells his corn.

The ears are
big and plump.

We help count.

We help carry.

The farmer thanks us
with plenty of corn.

We thank him with dinner!

Teachers Guide

Pre-Reading Activity

Brainstorm a list of things you might see on a farm. Then, as a class, sort the words into the following categories:

Living things (animate):	Nonliving things (inanimate):

Illustration © 2009 by Melissa Iwai

Comprehension Questions

1. Where are the children when they see the farm? Are there farms near where you live?

2. What is the farmer doing? What clues from the illustrations help you know?

3. What machine is the farmer using? Have you ever seen one work before?

4. What crop is the farmer planting? What clues from the text and illustrations make you think this?

5. Describe how the farmer feeds his plants. Why do you think this is important? Do all things that grow need to be fed? What do you like to be fed?

6. What is a seedling? Describe what it looks like.

7. Have you ever stopped by a farm? Why would you want to do that?

8. What is a stalk? What grows on a stalk?

9. Who picks the corn? Do you think picking corn is a hard or easy thing to do? Why?

10. Explain what happens at a farm stand. What clues did you use from the text and illustrations to answer?

11. What do the ears of corn look like? Do you like to eat corn on the cob?

12. Explain how the farmer and the family thank each other.

Vocabulary/Word Study

Add these high frequency words from the text to your word wall or create a board game (racetrack, snake, winding road) where students advance by being able to read and spell these words from the text:

> *we, by, a, the, is, and, are, to, his, us, of, with.*

WORD SORTS: Have students divide a sheet of paper in half lengthwise and then make two categories: one syllable words and two syllable words. List the following words on the board and have them sort the words into the correct category. (Decide whether you'd like them to work in pairs with a stronger reader paired with a developing one.) Or, put the words on index cards and have them take turns sorting the words in a learning center.

Words to sort: *we, drive, by, a, farm, the, farmer, plows, the, field, dirt, is, brown, bumpy, ride, plants, seeds, yellow, small, and, skip, feeds, plants, seedlings, green, soft, stop, waters, stalks, strong, tall, race, picks, corn, bins, full, heavy, walk, stand, sells, ears, big, plump, help, count, carry, thanks, plenty, dinner.*

One syllable words:	Two syllable words:

VOCABULARY: Have students fill out the following chart from the words in the story. Then, share with a reading partner.

New word:	I understood it in the story:	I think it means this:	I can make up a sentence with the word:
Plow			
Seedlings			
Stalks			
Heavy			
Plump			

Illustration © 2009 by Melissa Iwai

Tracie Vaughn Zimmer, author and literacy specialist, created this guide.

Book List

Ballet Stars
978-0-375-86909-9
GLB: 978-0-375-96909-6
Girl Interest • Rhyme & Alliteration
Art • Music & Theater

Bear Hugs
978-0-307-26113-7
Family & Relationships

Big Egg
978-0-679-88126-1
GLB: 978-0-679-98126-8
Humor • Family & Relationships • Animals

Boats
978-0-375-80221-8
Transportation • Rhyme & Alliteration

Cat Traps
978-0-679-86441-7
Humor • Animals

Chicks!
978-0-307-93221-1
GLB: 978-0-375-97117-4
Animals • Science & Nature

City Cats, Country Cats
978-0-307-26109-0
Fairy Tales & Fables

Corn Aplenty
978-0-375-85575-7
Science & Nature • Community • Concepts/Seasons

Dancing Dinos
978-0-307-26200-4
Rhyme & Alliteration • Humor • Dinosaurs

Dancing Dinos Go to School
978-0-375-83241-3
Rhyme & Alliteration • Dinosaurs • School

Dragon Egg
978-0-375-84350-1
GLB: 978-0-375-94350-8
Fairy Tales & Fables • Animals

Hog and Dog
978-0-375-83165-2
Animals • Friendship • Sports

Hot Dog
978-0-307-26101-4
Rhyme & Alliteration • Concepts/Words
Animals

I Like Bugs
978-0-307-26107-6
Science & Nature • Rhyme & Alliteration

I Like Stars
978-0-307-26105-2
Science & Nature • Rhyme & Alliteration

The Lion and the Mouse
978-0-679-88674-7
GLB: 978-0-679-98674-4
Fairy Tales & Fables • Classics • Animals

Monkey Play
978-0-375-86993-8
GLB: 978-0-375-96993-5
Animals • Humor • Rhyme & Alliteration

Sleepy Dog
978-0-394-86877-6
Animals • Bedtime Stories

The Snowball
978-0-679-86444-8
Rhyme & Alliteration • Concepts/Seasons

The Snowman
978-0-679-89443-8
Friendship • Christmas • Fantasy

Sunshine, Moonshine
978-0-679-86442-4
Bedtime Stories • Rhyme & Alliteration

Tae Kwon Do!
978-0-375-83448-6
Health/Nutrition/Physical Fitness • Sports
Asian/Asian American Interest

Too Many Dogs
978-0-679-86443-1 (0-679-86443-1)
Rhyme & Alliteration • Animals

Wheels!
978-0-679-86445-5
Transportation • Rhyme & Alliteration

Phonics Readers

Happy Alphabet!
978-0-375-81230-9
Rhyme & Alliteration • Concepts/Alphabet

Jack and Jill and Big Dog Bill
978-0-375-81248-4
Rhyme & Alliteration • Concepts/Words

Mouse Makes Words
978-0-375-81399-3
Rhyme & Alliteration • Concepts/Words

Mouse's Hide-and-Seek Words
978-0-375-82185-1
Rhyme & Alliteration • Concepts/Words

The Pup Speaks Up
978-0-375-81232-3
Animals • Rhyme & Alliteration • Friendship

Engage even the most reluctant readers with favorite characters!

Write-In Readers

Thomas Comes to Breakfast
978-0-375-82892-8
Transportation • Writing

Barbie

I Can Be a Horse Rider
978-0-375-97030-6
GLB: 978-0-307-93033-0
Media • Adventure • Friendship • Girl Interest

On Your Toes
978-0-375-83142-3
Activities, Crafts & Hobbies • Perseverance

Berenstain Bears

**The Berenstain Bears
Ride the Thunderbolt**
978-0-679-88718-8
Family & Relationships • Concepts/General
Activities, Crafts & Hobbies

**The Berenstain Bears'
Big Bear, Small Bear**
978-0-679-88717-1
Concepts/Shapes • Concepts/Opposites

We Like Kites
978-0-679-89231-1
Rhyme & Alliteration • Concepts/General

Disney

Best Dad in the Sea
978-0-7364-2131-7
Family & Relationships • Courage & Honor
Character Education/Caring

Big Bear, Little Bear
978-0-7364-2915-3
GLB: 978-0-7364-8108-3
Media • Fairy Tales & Fables • Animals
Family & Relationships • Adventure

The Blue Wish
978-0-307-93005-7
GLB: 978-0-375-97005-4
Media • Rhyme & Alliteration
Friendship • Adventure

Cinderella's Countdown to the Ball
978-0-7364-1225-4
Classics • Math • Concepts/Counting

Friends for a Princess
978-0-7364-2208-6
Fairy Tales & Fables • Rhyme & Alliteration
Friendship • Classics

Happy Birthday, Princess!
978-0-7364-2859-0
GLB: 978-0-7364-8099-4
Media • Fairy Tales & Fables
Girl Interest • Adventure

Just Keep Swimming
978-0-7364-2319-9
Self-Esteem • Animals

Me Too, Woody!
978-0-7364-1266-7
Friendship • Cooperation & Teamwork

Oh, Brother!
978-0-7364-2887-3
GLB: 978-0-7364-8114-4
Media • Fairy Tales & Fables • Animals
Family & Relationships • Adventure

Peter Pan
978-0-7364-3114-9
GLB: 978-0-7364-8135-9
Media • Adventure • Classics • Fantasy
Friendship

Run, Remy, Run!
978-0-7364-2476-9
Animals • Friendship

What Is a Princess?
978-0-7364-2238-3
Fairy Tales & Fables • Fantasy

**Peter Cottontale:
The Bunny Surprise**
978-0-7364-2857-6
GLB: 978-0-7364-8097-0
Media • Friendship • Humor • Adventure

Pocoyo

**Pocoyo:
Surprise for Pocoyo**
978-0-307-98099-1
GLB: 978-0-375-97134-1
Media • Friendship • Concepts/General
Adventure

Richard Scarry

**Richard Scarry's
Watch Your Step, Mr. Rabbit!**
978-0-679-88650-1
Humor • Cooperation & Teamwork

Sesame Street

Elmo Says Achoo!
978-0-375-80311-6
Humor • Friendship

Seuss

Cooking with the Cat
978-0-375-82494-4
Rhyme & Alliteration • Activities,
Crafts & Hobbies • Humor

Thomas the Tank Engine

Gordon's New View
978-0-375-83978-8
Transportation • Friendship

The Great Race
978-0-375-80284-3
Transportation • Friendship
Character Education/Sharing

Thomas and Percy and the Dragon
978-0-375-82230-8
GLB: 978-0-375-92230-5
Courage & Honor • Transportation
Character Education/Sharing

Thomas Goes Fishing
978-0-375-83118-8
Friendship • Transportation
Activities, Crafts & Hobbies

For more titles, visit StepIntoReading.com

Step into Reading, Random House, and the Random House colophon are registered trademarks of Random House, Inc.

Visit us on the Web!
StepIntoReading.com
randomhouse.com/kids

Educators and librarians, for a variety of teaching tools, visit us at RHTeachersLibrarians.com

ISBN: 978-0-7364-3027-2 (trade) — ISBN: 978-0-7364-8122-9 (lib. bdg.)

Manufactured in China   10 9 8 7 6 5 4 3 2 1

ALICE *in* WONDERLAND

Adapted by Pamela Bobowicz

Illustrated by the Disney Storybook Artists

Random House 🏠 New York

Alice was a young girl.

She liked to daydream.

She dreamed
of a strange land.

She wanted to go there.

A white rabbit ran by.
He looked at
his pocket watch.

"I'm late!"

he cried.

Alice ran after him.

The rabbit went
under a tree.

He went down a hole.

Alice followed.

She fell

down, down, down.

Alice was in
a strange forest.

She followed
the rabbit
to his house.

Alice went
into the house.
She ate some cookies.

The cookies made her
grow and grow.
She grew too big
for the house!

A dodo bird
gave her a carrot.
She ate the carrot.
It made her shrink!

Now Alice was smaller
than the bird.
The White Rabbit
ran away.

Alice searched for
the rabbit again.
She met some flowers.
They could talk!
They asked her what
kind of flower she was.

"I'm a girl, not a flower,"
Alice told them.

The flowers laughed.

Alice ran away.

Next Alice met
the Mad Hatter
and the March Hare.

They were having

a tea party.

The Mad Hatter
had a cake.
It was
under his hat!

He let Alice
make a wish.
She wished to find
the White Rabbit.

Alice was tired.
She could not find
the White Rabbit.
No one could help her.

Then Alice met a cat.
"I'm lost,"
she told him.

The cat asked Alice
where she wanted to go.
Alice didn't know.
"Then you're not lost!"
the cat said.

The cat led Alice
to a castle garden.

The White Rabbit
was there!
He worked for
the Queen of Hearts.

Alice wanted
to go home.
She told the Queen.

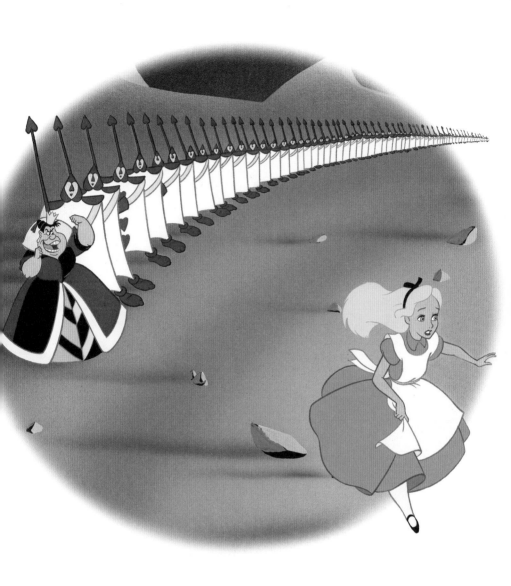

The Queen was angry.

Alice ran away.

Alice heard
her cat purring.
She opened her eyes.
She was home again.
It had all been a dream!

Teachers Guide

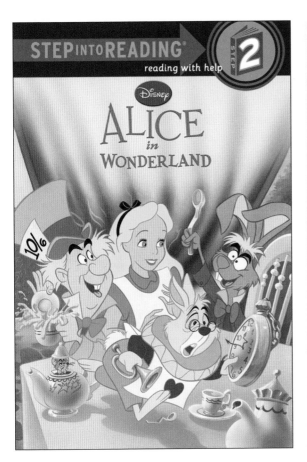

This guide meets the following common core standards:

KEY IDEAS AND DETAILS
1. Ask and answer questions about key details in a text.
2. Retell stories, including key details, and demonstrate understanding of their central message or lesson.
3. Describe characters, settings, and major events in a story, using key details.

INTEGRATION OF KNOWLEDGE AND IDEAS
7. Use illustrations and details in a story to describe its characters, setting, or events.

Pre-Reading Activity

Define the word *daydream* for the children: a dream that you have while you're awake. It is usually pleasant or fun, and often distracts you from what you should be doing.

Alice was a young girl who liked to daydream.

- **What do you like to daydream about?**

- **Do you think having an imagination and daydreaming are important or not? Why?**

Comprehension Questions

1. What did Alice like to do?

2. Who did Alice follow? Do you think it is safe to follow someone or not?

3. Explain what happened when Alice followed the rabbit under a tree.

4. Retell what happened when Alice ate some of the rabbit's cookies.

5. What effect did Alice experience after eating the carrot the dodo bird gave her?

6. Summarize what was said between Alice and the talking flowers.

7. Judge who you think is the strangest character Alice meets in her daydream.

8. Why do you think Alice wanted to follow the white rabbit so badly?

9. Explain why the cat told Alice that she was not lost. Where did he lead her?

10. Conclude why Alice ran from the Queen. How do the illustrations help you to know?

11. In the end, where had Alice been? Why do you think she dreamed of a cat?

12. Which illustration is your favorite? Why? Is it also your favorite part of the story?

Comprehension

Recreate this graphic organizer and you can have students fill it out for each book they read in **Step 1**:

The main character and their goal:	The setting of the story:	Three important events from the story:
		1.
		2.
		3.

Alice in Wonderland is often a child's first glimpse at a story with fantastical elements. Have children revisit the text and sort the words below into real and fantasy elements on the chart on the next page:

Alice, bluebird, butterfly, cat, white rabbit, pocket watch, the tree, the hole beneath it, forest, rabbit's house, dodo bird, carrot, rabbit's cookies, talking flowers, Mad Hatter, March Hare, cake under a hat, talking cat, castle garden, Queen, purring cat.

Real things:	Imaginary/Fantastical things:

Fluency

Repeated readings of a text have been shown to increase comprehension and fluency significantly. Set aside a small bit of time each day for students to read aloud in partners. Choose partners strategically with one advanced and one developing placed together. Don't forget to model appropriate listening and coaching strategies with pairs before beginning. Offer students a certificate (see next page) for being great reading partners to encourage the behavior you want others to model.

Draw a picture of the following words to show you understand what they mean, and then use each word in a sentence:

strange, daydream, follow, shrink, search, lost.

Illustration © 2012 by Disney Storybook Artists

Tracie Vaughn Zimmer, author and literacy specialist, created this guide.

CONGRATULATIONS!

This certificate certifies that

_____

and

_____

have demonstrated exceptional
reading partner conduct!

Book List

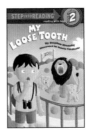

All Stuck Up
978-0-679-80216-7
Fairy Tales & Fables • Animals

Beef Stew
978-0-394-85046-7
Cooperation & Teamwork

Bones
978-0-679-89036-2
Science & Nature • Health/Nutrition/
Physical Fitness

Cat on the Mat
978-0-307-26207-3
Sports • Rhyme & Alliteration

David and the Giant
978-0-394-88867-5
Religious & Biblical Stories • Courage & Honor

Dinosaur Babies
978-0-679-81207-4
Science & Nature • Dinosaurs • Nonfiction

Mice Are Nice
978-0-679-88929-8
Animals • Rhyme & Alliteration

My Loose Tooth
978-0-679-88847-5
Rhyme & Alliteration • Health/Nutrition/
Physical Fitness

My New Boy
978-0-394-88277-2
Humor • Animals

Oh My, Pumpkin Pie!
978-0-375-82945-1
Concepts/Seasons • Rhyme & Alliteration

One Hundred Shoes
978-0-375-82178-3
Rhyme & Alliteration • Concepts/Counting • Math

Peanut
978-0-375-80618-6
Heroes & Heroism • Animals

P. J. Funnybunny's Bag of Tricks
978-0-375-82444-9
Family & Relationships

P. J. Funnybunny Camps Out
978-0-679-83269-0
Friendship • Humor

Platypus!
978-0-375-82417-3
Science & Nature • Animals/Nonfiction

Ready? Set. Raymond!
978-0-375-81363-4
Friendship • Black History Month
African/African American Interest

Sir Small and the Dragonfly
978-0-394-89625-0
Fantasy • Courage & Honor

The Statue of Liberty
978-0-679-86928-3
Nonfiction • History & Social Studies

The Teeny Tiny Woman
978-0-394-88320-5
Fairy Tales & Fables • Supernatural • Halloween

Tiger Is a Scaredy Cat
978-0-394-88056-3
Courage & Honor • Animals

Unicorn Wings
978-0-375-83117-1
GLB: 978-0-375-93117-8
Fairy Tales & Fables • Determination

Wake Up, Sun!
978-0-394-88256-7
Animals • Determination
Cooperation & Teamwork

Whose Feet?
978-0-375-82623-8
Animals • Science & Nature

Phonics Readers

Here Comes Silent E!
978-0-375-81233-0
GLB: 978-0-375-91233-7
Rhyme & Alliteration • Concepts/Words

Silly Sara
978-0-375-81231-6
Rhyme & Alliteration • Friendship

Math Readers

A Dollar for Penny
978-0-679-88973-1
Concepts/Counting • Family & Relationships
Math

Five Silly Fishermen
978-0-679-80092-7
Math • Concepts/Counting

Mary Clare Likes to Share
978-0-375-83421-9
Math • Concepts/Counting

Engage even the most reluctant readers with favorite characters!

Write-In Readers

Bear's Big Ideas
978-0-375-83391-5
Writing • Friendship • Cooperation

Berenstain Bears

The Berenstain Bears Catch the Bus
978-0-679-89227-4
Math • School • Family & Relationships
Concepts/Counting

The Berenstain Bears by the Sea
978-0-679-88719-5
GLB: 978-0-679-98719-2
Rhyme & Alliteration • Responsibility
Family & Relationships

Disney

Cinderella (Diamond)
978-0-7364-2888-0
GLB: 978-0-7364-8115-1
Media • Fairy Tales & Fables • Girl Interest
Adventure • Friendship

A Dream for a Princess
978-0-7364-2340-3
GLB: 978-0-7364-8044-4
Fairy Tales & Fables • Classics

Driving Buddies
978-0-7364-2339-7
Friendship • Self-Discovery

Game On
978-0-7364-2889-7
GLB: 978-0-7364-8116-8
Media • Humor • Technology and Computers
Adventure

Jewels for a Princess
978-0-7364-2908-5
GLB: 978-0-7364-8106-9
Media • Fairy Tales & Fables • Girl Interest
Adventure

Mater's Birthday Surprise
978-0-7364-2858-3
GLB: 978-0-7364-8098-7
Media • Adventure • Transportation
Boy Interest • Friendship

A Mother's Love
978-0-7364-2916-0
GLB: 978-0-7364-8109-0
Media • Fairy Tales & Fables • Animal
Family & Relationships • Adventure

A Pony for a Princess
978-0-7364-2045-7
GLB: 978-0-7364-8016-1
Friendship • Animals • Adventure

Sealed with a Kiss
978-0-7364-2363-2
Friendship • Animals

Surprise for a Princess
978-0-7364-2132-4
Family & Relationships • Humor

Here Comes Peter Cottontail
978-0-307-93032-3
GLB: 978-0-375-97031-3
Media • Character Education/Honesty
Responsibility, Friendship • Easter

Richard Scarry

Lowly Worm Meets the Early Bird
978-0-679-88920-5
GLB: 978-0-679-98920-2
Friendship • Animals • Animals
Humor • Growing Up

The Worst Helper Ever!
978-0-307-26100-7
Humor • Friendship

Sesame Street

Big Bird Says . . .
978-0-394-87499-9
Rhyme & Alliteration

Thomas the Tank Engine

Easter Engines
978-0-307-92996-9
GLB: 978-0-375-97003-0
Media • Transportation • Friendship
Adventure • Boy Interest • Easter

James Goes Buzz, Buzz
978-0-375-82860-7
Transportation • Perseverance

Henry and the Elephant
978-0-375-83976-4
Transportation • Animals

Happy Birthday, Thomas!
978-0-679-80809-1
Transportation • Emotions & Feelings

Secret of the Green Engine
978-0-307-93150-4
GLB: 978-0-375-97092-4
Media • Transportation • Adventure
Boy Interest • Friendship

Thomas and the School Trip
978-0-679-84365-8
Transportation • School • Perseverance

For my boy, Luther, and his buddy
Asher—it's fun watching you two
together. —C.M.H.

For my son, Ryan, who is learning to
eat his veggies. —B.S.

Text copyright © 2012 by Charise Mericle Harper
Cover and interior illustrations copyright © 2012 by Bob Shea

All rights reserved. Published in the United States by Random House Children's Books, a division of Random House, Inc., New York.

Step into Reading, Random House, and the Random House colophon are registered trademarks of Random House, Inc.

Visit us on the Web!
StepIntoReading.com
randomhouse.com/kids
Educators and librarians, for a variety of teaching tools, visit us at
randomhouse.com/teachers

Library of Congress Cataloging-in-Publication Data
Harper, Charise Mericle.
Wedgieman: a hero is born / by Charise Mericle Harper ; illustrated by Bob Shea.
p. cm. — (The adventures of Wedgieman)
Summary: Veggieboy practices flying, lifting, and helping people to hone his superhero skills, and finally Veggieman's training as a superhero is complete, but he is surprised when children want to change his name.
ISBN 978-0-307-93071-2 (trade paperback) — ISBN 978-0-375-97058-0 (Gibraltar library binding)
[1. Superheroes—Fiction. 2. Vegetables—Fiction. 3. Growth—Fiction.] I. Shea, Bob, ill. II. Title.
PZ7.H231323We 2012 [E]—dc23 2011016352

Manufactured in China   10 9 8 7 6 5 4 3 2 1

WEDGIEMAN: a HERO is BORN

The ADVENTURES of
WEDGIEMAN

By Charise Mericle Harper

Illustrated by Bob Shea

Random House 🏠 New York

One day a superhero was born.

His name was Veggiebaby,

and he was very hungry.

He ate vegetables, lots of them,

even the green ones.

The tiny round

ones were his

favorite.

There was a big sign on Veggiebaby's
wall. Veggiebaby looked at it.

"GAAAA!" said Veggiebaby.

He played with his food anyway.

He was good at it.

He made broccoli bears,

 tomato tigers,

spinach spiders,

and even giant
green-bean
gorillas.

Veggiebaby was brave.

He wasn't scared of vegetables, no
matter what they looked like.

He just drooled, looked
them in the eye,

and then gave them
a bite.
It was good training for
a superhero baby.

Babies are messy eaters.

Superhero babies are super-messy eaters.

When Veggiebaby ate lunch, there was food everywhere.

There were carrots covering the carpet.

There was squash on the sofa.

There were peas in his pants.

And sometimes, there was even

cabbage on the cat.

The cat did not like cabbage.

All the vegetables made Veggiebaby
very healthy.

He grew fast, and one day he turned
into Veggieboy.

Veggieboy said, "I must practice
my superhero skills."
He practiced flying.
It was not easy.

One day he spent nearly three hours
stuck on the ceiling.
It was a lot easier to go up than
to come down.

He practiced lifting.

He held a tree full of chattering
squirrels high in the air.

He held a bus full of chattering
grandmas high in the air.
"I can do more," said Veggieboy.
"Who wants to go next?"
Suddenly, there was silence.
Not everyone likes to look down
from the sky.

He practiced looking with his
X-ray eyes.

Not everyone was happy about that.

Not even Veggieboy.

Some things are better not seen.

He practiced
shape-shifting.

"I am a hamster!"
said Veggieboy.
Nothing
happened.

"I am a robot!"
said Veggieboy.

Nothing happened.

"I guess I can't
shape-shift,"
said Veggieboy.
He was only a little
bit unhappy.

Mostly, he was hungry.

He thought about carrots.

Suddenly, BAM!

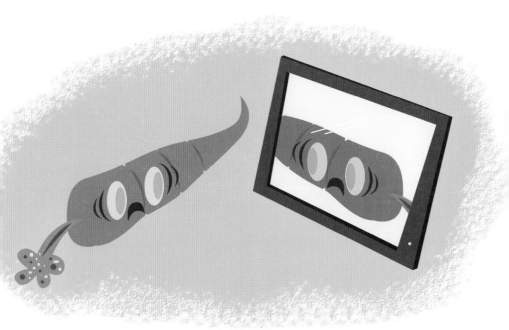

He was a giant carrot.

"Ah!" screamed Veggieboy.

"I look so tasty!"

He quickly changed back.

"That's dangerous!" said Veggieboy.

"I'm only going to use that
in emergencies."

Veggieboy was proud of his super-skills.

And because he was a super*hero*,

he only used them to do good.

On shopping days, he carried groceries
and old ladies.

He could find lost keys or missing socks.

And he was always helpful at fairs
and picnics.

Veggieboy was a very busy helper.

But there was one thing he never forgot.
He always ate his vegetables.

One day Veggieboy turned into
Veggieman.

Veggieman was now a grown-up.
"I need a new superhero outfit,"
he said.

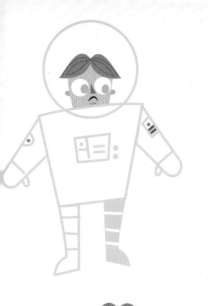

He went to the store.

He tried on lots of outfits.

Finally, he said, "I think this is the one. Now I can help the children of the world eat their veggies and be healthy!" He smiled and made a superhero pose in the mirror.

Suddenly, he heard a scream.

It was a cry for help.

"That's my call!" said Veggieman.

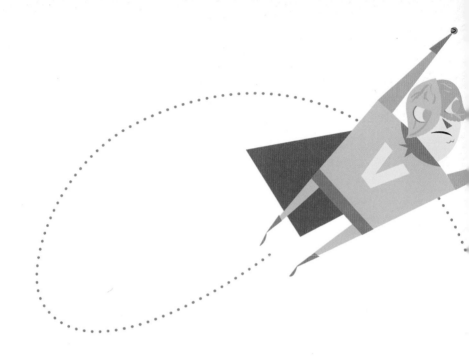

He ran out of the store and flew
into the sky.

Veggieman used his super-ears
to find the sound.
A small boy was stuck high in the
branches of a tree.
"Help me! Help me!"
cried the boy.

"Save him! Save him!"
cried the children
under the tree.

"Hang on!" shouted Veggieman.

He grabbed the boy and
carried him safely
to the ground.

"Eat your veggies and you can be strong like me," said Veggieman.

He gave the small boy some carrots.

All the children were happy.

"Yay! Wedgieman! Our hero!"

they cheered.

"No, wait," said Veggieman.

"It's *Veggie*man, not *Wedgie*man!"

"No it isn't!" said the small boy, and he pointed to Veggieman's chest.

A stick from the tree
was stuck to Veggieman's shirt.
It made his *V* look like a *W*.
Veggieman pulled off the stick.

"Silly children," he said. "It's a *V*,
 not a *W*. I'm Veggieman."

"I like Wedgieman better," said the boy.

"Yay! Wedgieman!" cheered the children.

Veggieman was confused.

He was not used to children.

Especially children who were wrong

but said they were right.

He thought for a moment

and then smiled.

He pointed to his chest.

"Look, children, even if I made this *V* into a *W*, it still wouldn't spell *wedgie*. And that's because *wedgie* has a *D* in it."

"That's okay," said the children.

"We don't care about spelling.

You can fix it."

And then they ran off to play.

THE END—OR IS IT?

Veggieman walked back to the store.
He was tired and
didn't feel like flying.

He was sorry that he didn't have any
extra carrots or spinach in his pockets.
"This outfit is too loose," he said.
"I need a smaller size."

He pulled up his pants.

A small boy was watching.

The small boy told everyone what
he had seen.

All the children were excited about the
new superhero in town.

His name was Wedgieman.

Teachers Guide

This guide meets the following common core standards:

READING: KEY IDEAS AND DETAILS

1. With prompting and support, ask and answer questions about key details in a text.
3. With prompting and support, identify characters, settings, and major events in a story.

CRAFT AND STRUCTURE

4. Ask and answer questions about unknown words in a text.

FLUENCY

4. Read emergent-reader texts with purpose and understanding.

Pre-Reading Activity

Show the kids the cover of the book and ask the following questions:

Who do you think the story will be about? Why? What clues did you use to make this prediction?

What makes a hero? Have you ever been a hero?

What types of powers do you think this character will have? Why?

Comprehension

Have students fill out the following graphic organizer about Wedgieman or any other **Step 3** title:

Who is the main character?	
What do they want?	
When does the story take place?	
Where is the setting of the story?	
Why are things hard for them?	
How do they solve their problem?	

Comprehension Questions

1. What naughty thing did Veggiebaby do when he was little?
2. How was Veggiebaby brave? Are you brave too?
3. Where did Veggiebaby's food end up? Why?
4. How did Veggiebaby turn into Veggieboy?
5. What types of things did Veggiebaby practice? Why?
6. How is the story introduced or started? How is the action over in the end?
7. If you could shapeshift, what would you become? Why?
8. Why was it dangerous for Veggieboy to become a carrot?
9. How does the illustration help you to understand the way Veggieboy was helpful at fairs and picnics? What did he do?
10. What types of outfits did Veggieman try on? Which one did he decide on? Why?
11. How did Veggieman save the boy stuck in the tree?
12. Explain how the kids became confused about his name.
13. Why did the children not care about spelling?
14. What did the boy see Veggieman do?
15. Predict what you think might happen after the story ends.

Vocabulary

New word:	What it means in my own words:	A picture that show it's meaning:
Brave		
Messy		
Chattering		
Practice		
Tasty		
Emergencies		
Groceries		

Fluency

Often students read word-by-word instead of reading in phrases which builds fluency. Project a piece of text (or a page from a Step 3 book) onto the board with a document camera or other device and then highlight the passage in phrases while the children watch and listen to you read it aloud. Then, as a class, practice reading the passage in phrases together. You might want to use the same text for a week. Poems and nursery rhymes are perfect for this because they are naturally phrased by line.

Tracie Vaughn Zimmer, author and literacy specialist, created this guide.

Book List

Abe Lincoln's Hat
978-0-679-84977-3
History & Social Studies • Biography &
Autobiography

Babe Ruth Saves Baseball!
978-0-375-83048-8
GLB: 978-0-375-93048-5
Biography & Autobiography • Sports
Black History Month

Baseball Ballerina
978-0-679-81734-5
Cooperation & Teamwork • Self-Esteem
Character Education/Sharing

Beans Baker's Best Shot
978-0-375-82839-3
Cooperation & Teamwork • Sports • Friendship

Bears: Life in the Wild
978-0-307-26303-2
Animals • Science & Nature • Nonfiction

**The Bravest Dog Ever: The True Story
of Balto**
978-0-394-89695-3
Nonfiction • Heroes & Heroism • Animals

Bully Trouble
978-0-394-84949-2
Friendship • Bullies

Christopher Columbus
978-0-679-80369-0
Biography & Autobiography
History & Social Studies

Daisy Jane, Best-Ever Flower Girl
978-0-375-83110-2
New Experiences • Friendship

Dinosaur Days
978-0-394-87023-6
Dinosaurs • Nonfiction

Dolphins!
978-0-679-84437-2
Science & Nature • Nonfiction • Animals

Eat My Dust!: Henry Ford's First Race
978-0-375-81510-2
Transportation • History & Social Studies
Biography & Autobiography

Fairies: A True Story!
978-0-375-86561-9
GLB: 978-0-375-96568-5
Fairy Tales & Fables, Girl Interest, History &
Social Studies • British Interest • Supernatural

The First Thanksgiving
978-0-679-80218-1
Thanksgiving • Nonfiction
History & Social Studies

**Francis Scott Key's
Star-Spangled Banner**
978-0-375-86725-5
GLB: 978-0-375-96725-2
Patriotism, Nonfiction, Biography &
Autobiography, History & Social Studies
War • Fourth of July

Fox and Crow Are Not Friends
978-0-375-86982-2
GLB: 978-0-375-96982-9
Animals • Fairy Tales & Fables • Humor

**George Washington and
the General's Dog**
978-0-375-81015-2
History & Social Studies • Fourth of July
Courage & Honor • Character Education/Honesty
Biography & Autobiography • Animals/Nonfiction

Gorillas: Gentle Giants of the Forest
978-0-679-87284-9
Science & Nature • Nonfiction Animals/Nonfiction

The Great Tulip Trade
978-0-375-82573-6
Historical Fiction • Family & Relationships

Hungry, Hungry Sharks
978-0-394-87471-5
Science & Nature • Nonfiction
Animals/Nonfiction

Johnny Appleseed: My Story
978-0-375-81247-7
Patriotism • Myths, Legends & Folklore
History & Social Studies

**Lewis and Clark:
A Prairie Dog for President**
978-0-375-81120-3
Humor • Historical Fiction • Animals

Little Witch Goes to School
978-0-679-88738-6
Humor • School • Family & Relationships
Back to School

Little Witch Learns to Read
978-0-375-82179-0
Family & Relationships • Determination
Back to School

Little Witch's Big Night
978-0-394-86587-4
Humor • Halloween • Character Education/Sharing

**Listen Up!: Alexander Graham Bell's
Talking Machine**
978-0-375-83115-7
Biography & Autobiography • History & Social
Studies • Character Education

The Missing Tooth
978-0-394-89279-5
Growing Up • Friendship

Molly the Brave and Me
978-0-394-84175-5
Friendship • Courage & Honor

Monster Bugs
978-0-679-86974-0
Science & Nature • Animals/Nonfiction
Nonfiction

Motorcyles
978-0-375-84116-3
GLB: 978-0-375-94116-0
Transportation • Nonfiction

Norma Jean, Jumping Bean
978-0-394-88668-8
Friendship • Acceptance & Belonging

The Nutcracker Ballet
978-0-679-82385-8
Classics • Christmas • Art, Music & Theater

Pretty Penny Comes Up Short
978-0-375-86978-5
GLB: 978-0-375-96978-2
Making Choices • Responsibility • Girl Interest

Pirate Mom
978-0-375-83323-6
GLB: 978-0-375-93323-3
Humor • Family & Relationships
Acceptance & Belonging

Samantha the Snob
978-0-679-84640-6
Friendship • Acceptance & Belonging

S-S-Snakes!
978-0-679-84777-9
Animals • Nonfiction

Trains!
978-0-375-86941-9
GLB: 978-0-375-96941-6
Transportation • Boy Interest • Technology
and Computers

Tentacles! Tales of the Giant Squid
978-0-375-81307-8
Science & Nature • Nonfiction • Myths,
Legends & Folklore • Animals/Nonfiction

The Stinky Giant
978-0-375-86743-9
GLB: 978-0-375-96743-6
Science & Nature • Humor • Fairy Tales & Fables

The True Story of Pocahontas
978-0-679-86166-9
Native American Interest • History & Social
Studies • Biography & Autobiography

Wedgieman: A Hero Is Born
978-0-307-93071-2
GLB: 978-0-375-97058-0
Heroes & Heroism • Humor
Health/Nutrition/Physical Fitness

Wedgieman to the Rescue
978-0-307-93072-9
GLB: 978-0-375-97059-7
Humor • Heroes & Heroism
Health/Nutrition/Physical Fitness

Whales: The Gentle Giants
978-0-394-89809-4
Nonfiction • Science & Nature
Animals/Nonfiction

Wild, Wild Wolves
978-0-679-81052-0
Animals/Nonfiction • Science & Nature
Nonfiction

Math Readers

The Dragon's Scales
978-0-679-88381-4
Math • Concepts/Counting

Write-In Readers

Miss Grubb, Super Sub!
978-0-375-82894-2
School • Humor • Writing

Engage even the most reluctant readers with favorite characters!

Arthur

Arthur and the School Pet
978-0-375-81001-5
GLB: 978-0-375-91001-2
School • Animals • Responsibility

Arthur Lost in the Museum
978-0-375-82973-4
Art, Music & Theater • Friendship

Arthur Tricks the Tooth Fairy
978-0-679-88464-4
Health/Nutrition/Physical Fitness
Family & Relationships

Arthur's Classroom Fib
978-0-375-82975-8
GLB: 978-0-375-92975-5
Character Education/Honesty • School

Arthur's Fire Drill
978-0-679-88476-7
Safety & Security • Humor

Arthur's Lost Puppy
978-0-679-88466-8
Family & Relationships • Animals

Arthur's Reading Race
978-0-679-86738-8
Concepts/Words • School

Ironman Armored Adventures

The Crimson Dynamo Returns!
978-0-375-96178-6
GLB: 978-0-375-86178-9
Media • Adventure • Good vs. Evil

Disney

The Incredible Dash
978-0-7364-2265-9
Good vs. Evil • Heroes & Heroism
Family & Relationships • Adventure

The Perfect Pumpkin Hunt
978-0-7364-2847-7
GLB: 978-0-7364-8094-9
Media • Fairy Tales & Fables • Girl Interest
Adventure • Friendship

Richard Scarry

The Best Mistake Ever!
And Other Stories
978-0-394-86816-5
Short Stories & Anthologies • Determination

For more titles, visit StepIntoReading.com

For Katie Claire Gisondi & Jack Gisondi,
two unforgettable little treats
—F.M.

To Mary, with love
—R.W.

Author acknowledgments: Thanks to Bryan Craig, research librarian at Monticello, for his expertise. Thanks to my talented editor and collaborator, Shana Corey, for her patience and creativity. Thanks to Angela Roberts for her assistance. And thanks to Mark Klein for finding that apple picker!

Photo credits: Portrait of Thomas Jefferson © Burstein Collection/CORBIS. Macaroni-making machine courtesy of the Library of Congress.

www.stepintoreading.com

Educators and librarians, for a variety of teaching tools, visit us at
www.randomhouse.com/teachers

Library of Congress Cataloging-in-Publication Data
Murphy, Frank.
Thomas Jefferson's feast / by Frank Murphy ; illustrated by Richard Walz.
   p.   cm. — (Step into reading. A step 4 book)
SUMMARY: Tells of Thomas Jefferson's trip to France in 1784, and all the exotic foods he learned about and then introduced to America, including ice cream, macaroni and cheese, and tomatoes.
ISBN 0-375-82289-5 (trade) — ISBN 0-375-92289-X (lib. bdg.)
1. Jefferson, Thomas, 1743–1826—Juvenile literature.   2. Jefferson, Thomas, 1743–1826—Journeys—France—Juvenile literature.   3. Presidents—United States—Biography—Juvenile literature.   4. Food—History—18th century—Juvenile literature.   5. Cookery, French—History—18th century—Juvenile literature.   [1. Jefferson, Thomas, 1743–1826.   2. Presidents. 3. Food—History.]   I. Walz, Richard, ill.   II. Title.   III. Series: Step into reading. Step 4 book.
E332.79 .M87   2003   394.1'0973—dc21   2002014219

Manufactured in China
10 9 8 7 6 5 4 3 2 1

STEP INTO READING, RANDOM HOUSE, and the Random House colophon are registered trademarks of Random House, Inc.

Thomas Jefferson's
FEAST

by Frank Murphy
illustrated by Richard Walz

Random House 🏠 New York

Long ago, before your great-great-grandparents were born, there lived a man named Thomas Jefferson. You probably know his name because he was the third president of the United States.

But that's not all there is to know about Thomas Jefferson.

Thomas Jefferson loved to read.
He collected books about the stars and
books about history. In fact, he had one of
the largest libraries in America.

Thomas Jefferson also loved to write.

He wrote letters to people like Benjamin Franklin and George Washington. In his lifetime, he wrote over *20,000* letters. That's like writing a letter a day, every day, for 55 years!

Many of Thomas's letters said that America should be its own country. (The British thought America belonged to them.)

So Thomas Jefferson went to work writing the Declaration of Independence. He wrote and rewrote it for 17 days straight—until he got it just right.

Of course, with all that reading and writing and thinking, sometimes Thomas Jefferson got tired.

Sometimes his back hurt.

And sometimes he got hungry. When that happened . . .

. . . he usually took a break and had a snack. Because Thomas Jefferson really, *really* loved food!

Thomas liked food *so* much, he
sometimes spent as much as 50 dollars
on groceries in just one day! (That would
be like spending *750* dollars today!)

Thomas also spent a lot of time *thinking* about food. He even thought about better ways to get food!

Sometimes Thomas Jefferson got hungry late at night after everyone else had gone to bed.

When that happened, he had to tiptoe down the hallway and all the way downstairs to the kitchen.

Then he had to fix a tray of food and carry it *all* the way back upstairs and down the long, dark hallway to the dining room.

If he was lucky, there was still a little left when he sat down to eat.

Thomas needed an easier way to get his food upstairs.

So he built a little elevator in his house. It was too small to carry people. But it could take food and drinks from the kitchen to the dining room upstairs—without spilling a drop! Thomas called his invention a dumbwaiter.

Thomas's dumbwaiter is still in his house in Virginia today—and it *still* works!

Thomas had a giant garden behind his house. The garden was 1,000 feet long. It was filled with more than 200 different kinds of fruits and vegetables.

If you visit Thomas's house, Monticello, today, you can still see many of the fruit trees he planted.

Sometimes Thomas wanted a snack from his garden. But the apples on the bottoms of the trees were usually already picked.

"Hmmm," thought Thomas. "There must be a simple way to get apples from the tops of the trees."

Thomas found a long wooden pole. He attached a metal basket to it. The basket had hooks at the top.

He used the hooks to pull off the apples. Presto! Ripe apples fell into the basket!

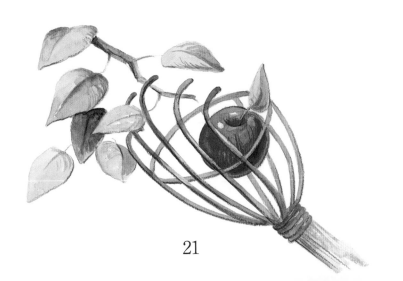

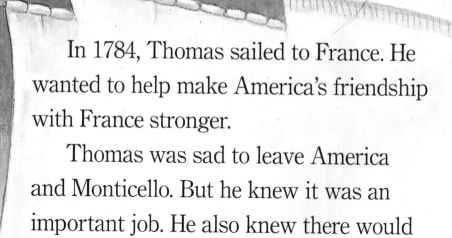

In 1784, Thomas sailed to France. He wanted to help make America's friendship with France stronger.

Thomas was sad to leave America and Monticello. But he knew it was an important job. He also knew there would be *lots* of new foods to try!

Thomas was right!

In between meetings, he tasted macaroni covered with cheese!

He munched on potatoes fried in the
French manner.

One night, he went to a dinner party.
"Hello!" said Thomas.
"Bonjour!" said his host. (*Bonjour*
means "hello" in French.)

Thomas's host offered him a special
dessert. It was ice cream wrapped in a
warm pie crust. Ice cream hadn't come to
America yet.

For *bonjour,* say: bohn-JOOR

Thomas took a bite.

"Good!" said Thomas.

"*Bon!*" said his host. (*Bon* means "good" in French.)

For *bon*, say: bohn

During his visit, Thomas saw a
Frenchman eating a bright red fruit.
It was called a *pomme d'amour*. (That
means "love apple" in French.) Thomas
had seen the fruit before. But in America
it was usually just used for decoration.
Most people thought it was poison, so no
one ate it.

The Frenchman promised it was not
poison. So Thomas took a bite.

Thomas *loved* the love apple!

For *pomme d'amour*, say: pohm dah-MOOR

Thomas stayed in France for five years. When it was time for him to go back to America, he couldn't wait to share all his new favorite foods!

He wrote down the recipes for macaroni and cheese, fried potatoes, and ice cream. He even decided to plant some love apples at Monticello.

He waved goodbye to his French friends and got on the ship.

"*Au revoir!*" he said. (*Au revoir* means "goodbye" in French.)

For *au revoir*, say: oh ruh-VWAHR

"How was France?" everyone asked when Thomas got home.

"Delicious!" answered Thomas.

He decided to have a feast to show off the new foods.

Of course, that was easier said than done.

Thomas planted love apple seeds—

and waited for them to grow.

He drew a picture of a macaroni-
making machine he had seen in France.
Then he sent a friend all the way to Italy
to buy one. (Thomas had heard that Italy
had the best macaroni-making machines!)

He dug up potatoes from his garden.

Finally, he made ice cream. This was *not* easy. First he mixed cream and eggs and sugar. He packed it with ice and salt.

Then he stirred and stirred *and stirred.*

At last, everything was ready. The love apples were ripe. The macaroni was cheesy. The potatoes were crisp. The ice cream was icy.

"Perfect!" said Thomas.

Thomas invited all his friends.

"What's for dinner?" they asked.

"It's a surprise," said Thomas. "Let's eat!"

Thomas's guests loved the feast! They gobbled up the macaroni and cheese. They ate every last fried potato. They asked for more of Thomas's ice cream. They even asked for the recipes.

When they were about to go home,
Thomas noticed something. No one had
touched their love apples! Everyone
believed they were poison.

"Try them," Thomas begged.

"No thanks," everyone said. "We're full."

Thomas felt terrible! How could he get
people to try love apples?

The next day Thomas rode into the town of Lynchburg to visit a friend. He noticed a few love apples growing in her yard. Suddenly, Thomas had an idea!

He asked if he could pick a few love apples. His friend said yes.

Thomas walked down the street with the love apples.

He raised one to his mouth. People stopped and pointed. "What are you doing?" they shouted. "That's poison! Stop!"

Thomas took a bite.

"Oh no!" everyone said. "Save him! He's going to get sick!"

But Thomas didn't get sick.

He just kept eating.

Pretty soon, people got curious about the love apples. They tried them themselves. *"Scrumptious!"* everyone said.

And to this day, Americans enjoy eating love apples. (Especially on pizza!)

Today, we still eat many of the foods Thomas Jefferson brought from France. Only now we call "potatoes fried in the French manner" French fries. And we call love apples tomatoes!

(Macaroni and cheese is still called macaroni and cheese, and ice cream is still called ice cream!)

AUTHOR'S NOTE

Thomas Jefferson stayed in France from 1784 to 1789. He may not have served all the foods in this book at one party. But he really did introduce them to America. And he was well known for his fancy dinner parties. So it just may have happened this way.

Thomas Jefferson also really did have a pet mockingbird that flew around his study. His name was Dick.

Thomas Jefferson

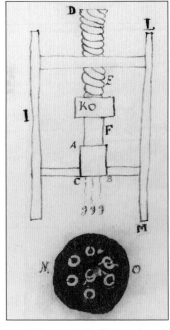

Thomas Jefferson's drawing of a macaroni-making machine

Teachers Guide

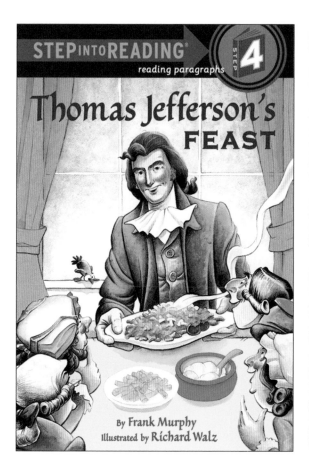

STEPINTO**READING** reading paragraphs 4

Thomas Jefferson's FEAST

By **Frank Murphy**
Illustrated by **Richard Walz**

This guide meets the following common core standards:

TEXT TYPES AND PURPOSES
1. Write opinion pieces on topics or texts, supporting a point of view with reasons.

FLUENCY
4. Use context to confirm or self-correct word recognition and understanding, rereading as necessary.

INFORMATIONAL TEXT— KEY IDEAS AND DETAILS
1. Ask and answer questions to demonstrate understanding of a text, referring explicitly to the text as the basis for the answers.
3. Describe the relationship between a series of historical events, scientific ideas or concepts, or steps in technical procedures in a text, using language that pertains to time, sequence, and cause/effect.

Pre-Reading Activity

In pairs, have students fill out the first two columns in the chart before reading the book. Then, have them complete the final column after reading it together.

What I KNOW about Thomas Jefferson:	What I WANT to KNOW about Thomas Jefferson:	What I LEARNED about Thomas Jefferson:

Vocabulary/Word Work

A word in context:	What I think it means:	After I check a source:
In his lifetime, he wrote over 20,000 letter.		
Thomas called his invention a dumbwaiter.		
He used the hooks to pull off the apples. Presto! Ripe apples fell into the basket!		
He munched on potatoes fried in the French manner.		
But in America it was usually just used for decoration. Most people thought that it was poison, so no one ate it.		

Comprehension

Have students find a key quote from the text that proves the following facts about Thomas Jefferson.

Important fact about Thomas Jefferson:	Where the proof appears in the story:
Thomas Jefferson was once the president of the United States.	
Thomas Jefferson bought lots of books.	
Thomas Jefferson revised his writing to make it better.	
Thomas Jefferson liked to eat.	
Thomas Jefferson was an inventor.	
Thomas Jefferson did not always live in Virginia.	
Thomas Jefferson convinced people to try tomatoes.	

Cause & Effect

In pairs, have students match the following causes and effects.

CAUSES:	EFFECTS:
Thomas Jefferson really loved food.	Jefferson created a dumbwaiter.
Thomas Jefferson hated carrying his food up the stairs.	He introduced his friends to many French foods.
Thomas Jefferson loved to write letters.	Jefferson wrote 20,000 letters in his lifetime.
He tried many new foods in France.	Thomas Jefferson proved love apples were safe.
He couldn't reach the apples high on his fruit trees.	He invented a device that could pick apples off the top of a tree.
People thought love apples were poisonous in America.	He once spent over $50 on food for just one day.

Writing

Have children write a persuasive letter to a friend about which book they should read next. They must give at least three reasons as to why their friend would like the book without revealing the ending.

Illustration © 2003 by Richard Walz

Tracie Vaughn Zimmer, author and literacy specialist, created this guide.

Book List

Choppers!
978-0-375-82517-0
Transportation • Nonfiction

Dactyls! Dragons of the Air
978-0-375-83013-6
Nonfiction • Dinosaurs

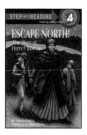

Escape North!
The Story of Harriet Tubman
978-0-375-80154-9
Courage & Honor • Nonfiction • Black History
Month • Biography & Autobiography
African/African American Interest

First Kids
978-0-375-82218-6
Patriotism • Nonfiction • History & Social Studies

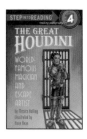

The Great Houdini
978-0-679-88573-3
Biography & Autobiography • Nonfiction
History & Social Studies

Helen Keller: Courage in the Dark
978-0-679-87705-9
Biography & Autobiography • Courage & Honor
Nonfiction

Hungry Plants
978-0-375-82533-0
Science & Nature • Nonfiction

How Not to Babysit Your Brother
978-0-375-82856-0
Family & Relationships • Humor • Character
Education/Responsibility

How Not to Start Third Grade
978-0-375-83904-7
School • Humor • Back to School

Ice Mummy: The Discovery of
a 5,000 Year-old Man
978-0-679-85647-4
Nonfiction • History & Social Studies

Han Christian Andersen's
The Little Mermaid
978-0-679-82241-7
Adventure • Self-Discovery • Love & Romance
Family & Relationships

The Mystery of the Pirate Ghost
978-0-394-87220-9
Mystery & Suspense

No Tooth, No Quarter!
978-0-394-84956-0
Humor • Health/Nutrition/Physical Fitness

Pompeii . . . Buried Alive!
978-0-394-88866-8
Ancient Worlds • Nonfiction • Science & Nature
History & Social Studies

Soccer Sam
978-0-394-88406-6
Sports • Hispanic/Hispanic American Interest
Friendship

Thomas Jefferson's Feast
978-0-375-82289-6
Biography & Autobiography • Historical
Fiction/Colonial America • Historical Fiction
Humor

The Titanic: Lost . . . and Found
978-0-394-88669-5
Nonfiction • History & Social Studies

Tut's Mummy: Lost . . . and Found
978-0-394-89189-7
Ancient Worlds • Nonfiction
History & Social Studies

20,000 Baseball Cards Under the Sea
978-0-679-81569-3
Humor • Science Fiction • Adventure

Volcanoes! Mountains of Fire
978-0-679-88641-9
Science & Nature • Nonfiction

Wild Cats
978-0-375-82551-4
Science & Nature • Nonfiction
Animals/Nonfiction

Math Readers

Ben Franklin and the Magic Squares
978-0-375-80621-6
Biography & Autobiography
Concepts/Mathematics • History & Social Studies

The Fly on the Ceiling
978-0-679-88607-5
Biography & Autobiography
Concepts/Mathematics • History & Social Studies

Engage even the most reluctant
readers with favorite characters!

Seuss

Do Not Open This Crate!
978-0-375-82488-3
Rhyme & Alliteration • Humor
Cooperation & Teamwork

**Teenage Mutant Ninja Turtles
Green Team!**
978-0-307-98070-0
GLB: 978-0-375-97146-4
Media • Adventure • Friendship • Boy Interest

For more titles, visit StepIntoReading.com

Step 4 Book List

For Luke Easter, from a fan
—J.O'C.

For Roberto Clemente
—J.B.

Photo credits: pp. 9, 38 (top left), AP/Wide World Photos; cover, Hulton Archive/Getty Images; pp. 1, 26, 29, 32, 38 (bottom right), 47, National Baseball Library, Cooperstown, N.Y.; pp. 14–15, 38 (bottom left and top right), courtesy of National Baseball Library; p. 41, UPI/Bettmann Newsphotos.

www.stepintoreading.com

Educators and librarians, for a variety of teaching tools, visit us at www.randomhouse.com/teachers

Library of Congress Cataloging-in-Publication Data
O'Connor, Jim.
Jackie Robinson and the story of all-black baseball / by Jim O'Connor ; illustrated by Jim Butcher.
   p. cm. — (Step into reading. A step 5 book)
SUMMARY: Presents a biography of the first black baseball player to play in the major leagues when he joined the Brooklyn Dodgers in 1947. Also traces the history of all-black baseball teams.
ISBN 0-394-82456-3 (trade) — ISBN 0-394-92456-8 (lib. bdg.)
1. Robinson, Jackie, 1919–1972—Juvenile literature.
2. Baseball players—United States—Biography—Juvenile literature.
3. African American baseball players—Biography—Juvenile literature.
4. Baseball—United States—History—Juvenile literature.
5. Negro leagues—United States—History—Juvenile literature. [1. Robinson, Jackie, 1919–1972. 2. Baseball players. 3. African Americans—Biography.] I. Butcher, Jim, ill. II. Title. III. Series: Step into reading. Step 5 book.
GV865.R6027 2003 796.357'092—dc21 2002153806

Manufactured in China

JACKIE ROBINSON

AND THE STORY OF
ALL-BLACK BASEBALL

by Jim O'Connor
illustrated by Jim Butcher

Random House 🏠 New York

1

Jackie Makes History

April 15, 1947

It is opening day at Ebbets Field, the home of the Brooklyn Dodgers. Today they are playing the Boston Braves. The crowd is excited. The crowd is always excited on opening day. But this day is special for another reason.

All along the third-base line fans peer across the bright green diamond. They try to see the new player that the whole country has been talking about.

He is over in the Dodgers' dugout. He sits by himself. He looks nervous, and his teammates leave him alone.

Soon the announcer begins to call out the Dodgers' names. One by one the players run out onto the field. The stands erupt with a deafening roar. Finally the new player's name is called. Someone pats him on the back. Then he jogs to first base with a funny pigeon-toed stride that soon will be famous everywhere.

Who is this player? And why is this day so special?

He is Jackie Robinson. He's twenty-seven years old. And he's just become the first black man to play major-league baseball in the twentieth century.

Today about a quarter of all major-league ballplayers are black. But in 1947 the world is a very different place. Many hotels will not give rooms to black people. Many restaurants will not serve food to black people. In the South there are separate schools for white children and black children. Even

drinking fountains have signs. They say "For whites only."

For more than fifty years major-league baseball has been for whites only too. But not anymore. Not with Jackie Robinson in the Dodger lineup.

Black fans have their hopes riding on Jackie. They know it is not easy being the first man to cross the "color line" in baseball.

During the season Jackie is booed by people in the stands. They call him awful names. They tell him to go back to the cotton fields, where he belongs.

On the field it isn't any better. Pitchers throw bean balls—balls aimed right at Jackie's head. Runners try to spike him with the sharp cleats on their shoes.

At home he gets hate mail. There are letters that threaten to kill him, beat up his wife, and kidnap their baby son.

The pressure gets to Jackie. After only a

few games he falls into a batting slump. He makes an out twenty times before getting a hit.

But Jackie doesn't quit. It is hard to take the insults without fighting back. It is hard to be "the first." But he knows one thing. If other black players are to get a chance in the big leagues, he has to keep quiet and keep playing.

Jackie pulls out of his slump and starts showing what he's got. By the end of the season he is hitting .296. He leads the Dodgers in runs scored and stolen bases. He has belted twelve home runs—the most any Dodger has hit this season.

With every hit, with every stolen base, with every run scored, Jackie wins more fans. Wherever the Dodgers play, the stands are packed with people who want to see Jackie. There is even a train just for fans going to some Dodgers-Reds games in Cincinnati. It is called the Jackie Robinson Special.

By the middle of the season other teams start signing up black players too. It is the beginning of the end for whites-only baseball.

But it's the beginning of the end for all-black baseball too.

For nearly seventy years there have been professional all-black baseball teams. They have never been allowed in the major leagues. But they have had their own leagues. The Negro leagues. Up to now they have given thousands of black players their only chance to play pro baseball. But now all that is changing. As the big stars of black baseball sign up with major-league teams, the Negro leagues grow weaker. Fans stop coming to the games.

Fourteen years after Jackie Robinson's first game with the Dodgers, the Negro leagues are wiped out. A forgotten chapter in baseball history.

2

Barnstorming

Pro baseball was born soon after the Civil War. For the first time men started playing baseball for a living. Not just for fun. In those early days there were a few black players on different teams. They were good—just as good as their white teammates. But they always got cut or traded. All because of the color of their skin.

Bud Fowler was the first black to play pro baseball. People who saw him said he was a great second baseman. But no club would keep him. One season he was on five different teams.

The story goes that it was Bud Fowler who invented shin guards. Before a game he would tape pieces of wood around his lower legs. It was the only way he could protect himself from all the players who tried to spike him.

Bud Fowler once said, "The color of my skin is against me." And he was right.

By 1899 black players were completely shut out of pro baseball. No team owners would hire them. But that didn't stop black players—they started up teams of their own.

The first all-black team was called the Cuban Giants. It was started by a group of waiters at a hotel in Babylon, New York. Nobody on the team was really Cuban. But during games they pretended to speak Spanish. They did this because they thought white fans would come to see Cubans play. Even Cubans with very dark skin. But they were afraid no white fans would ever watch ordinary black Americans play baseball.

Right away the Cuban Giants were a hit with black fans. At last they had a team they could root for. Soon more black teams sprang up. Because the Cuban Giants were so popular, other teams used Giants in their name too. There were the Leland Giants. The Columbia Giants. There was even a team called the Cuban X Giants!

Nearly all the black teams were from big cities. Places like New York, Chicago, Philadelphia, Pittsburgh. Sometimes the black teams played games against each other. But

they did not belong to a real league that set up games for them. Not like the big all-white teams. Most of the time the black clubs just traveled on a team bus from town to town, looking for a game wherever they could find one. This was called barnstorming.

Barnstorming brought really great baseball to out-of-the-way places. Back then there was no TV. The only way to see a baseball game was to *be* at a baseball game. And America in those days was really baseball crazy. It was the number one sport. So when a good black team arrived in a small town, it was like a holiday. Factories might shut down early. Schools sometimes closed for half a day. The whole town—blacks and whites—would turn out to see the black team play ball!

Barnstorming meant spending weeks on the road. It was a hard way of life. Especially in the South. Often no hotels or restaurants let in blacks. So the teams had to eat and sleep right on their bus. Sometimes in warm weather they slept by the side of the road. Sometimes they even slept on the bleachers at the ball fields.

Barnstorming meant playing in all kinds of places. One day a team might play in a real ballpark with stands and a scoreboard. The next day they might play in a school-yard. Or even a cow pasture! That didn't bother the black teams. They were pros. And they would play wherever there were paying fans.

Most of all barnstorming meant playing lots and lots of baseball. To make enough money, teams squeezed in two and even three games a day. Sunset was the only thing that stopped them. After all, they couldn't play in the dark. And once good electric lights came into use, darkness didn't stop them either! Black teams were the first, in fact, to play night games. They just brought big lights along with them.

Then, after the last inning was over, down came the lights and the tired players would climb back on their bus. It was time to head for the next town and the next game.

Barnstorming was too tough a life for some players. After a season or two they quit baseball.

But most players stayed on the road for as long as they could. They made pretty good money at a time when black people often had trouble getting any kind of job. Maybe they weren't in the major leagues. But they did have lots of fans—black *and* white fans. And when they put on their uniforms and ran out onto the field, they were doing what they loved best. Playing baseball.

3

"Smart Baseball"

Nobody ever did more for black baseball than a man named Rube Foster. He wanted black baseball to be just as well run, just as well respected, as the major leagues. And he spent nearly his whole life trying to make it that way.

Rube started out in 1907 as a pitcher for a team in Chicago called the Leland Giants. He was a good baseball player. But he turned out to be an even better baseball manager.

In 1911 Rube started up a new team called the Chicago American Giants. And what a team it was. Rube got all the best black players of the day. But he knew it took more than raw talent to make a powerhouse of a club.

Most black teams did not get a lot of coaching. There was no time for that on the road. Players just joined a team and went out and played. But Rube drilled his team in what he called "smart baseball."

Black baseball was a lot different from white baseball. White baseball came to depend on home-run hitters like Babe Ruth to win games. But black baseball did not.

On black teams pitchers were allowed to throw all kinds of tricky pitches. They could throw a spitball. They could throw a "shine ball." That meant the ball had a little Vaseline rubbed on it. Pitchers could also nick or scratch the ball. That made it jump and dip on the way to the plate.

This kind of pitching made it harder to hit a homer. So Rube made his players work on getting a piece of the ball. That meant getting a base hit. In this kind of game bunting was very important. So Rube sometimes put a hat inside the baselines. He made his players learn to bunt right into it!

Rube wanted players who were fast runners, players who stole lots of bases. This made the games exciting. And it brought the American Giants lots of victories.

Rube was from Texas and called everybody "darlin'." But any player who didn't listen to Rube was in BIG trouble. During games Rube always sat smoking a pipe. He used his pipe to give signals to the players. If he puffed it one way, that meant the batter should bunt. If he puffed it another way, that meant the man at first should steal second.

And that's just what the players would do if they wanted to stay with the American Giants.

Rube wanted a real baseball home for his team, even though hardly any black teams had stadiums of their own. When black teams played in a big city, they had to rent a ballpark from a major-league team. They had to pay a lot of money, and they could only play there while the major-league team was out of town. Sometimes the black teams weren't even allowed to use the showers or the locker rooms. That wasn't good enough for Rube. He saw to it that a stadium was built for his team. It could seat 9,000 people.

All of Rube's hard work paid off. The American Giants were so popular that sometimes they drew bigger crowds than the Cubs or the White Sox—Chicago's two major-league teams—when all three teams were playing on the same day.

Rube hoped to have a team that was so good, the whole team would be asked to join the major leagues. It would be the first black major-league club. That didn't happen. But in 1920 Rube did start a league for the best black teams of the day. It was called the Negro National League. It set up games between teams. And it set down rules for players.

But then in 1926 Rube Foster got very sick. He had to retire from baseball. He died in 1930. And two years later his league died too.

Did this mean the end of black baseball? Far from it. The 1930s and 1940s became the golden age of black baseball. And the super-star of this golden age was a pitcher with an arm of iron. A man named Satchel Paige.

4
The Great Satchel

No pitcher in the history of baseball can match Satchel Paige. Usually pitchers wear out faster than other players. Their arms go from so much throwing. But Satchel was never your usual pitcher. His career stretched over forty years and thousands of games. He was around sixty when he finally stopped pitching!

LeRoy Paige was born in Alabama sometime in the early 1900s. No one, including Satchel, was ever sure of his exact birthday. He got his nickname when he was just a little boy. He used to earn extra money carrying people's satchels at the train station.

In 1924 Satchel pitched his first pro game for the Mobile Tigers. It was the first of about two hundred and fifty teams Satchel played for.

Satchel was tall and thin. Almost skinny. But when he reared back and threw the ball, he was throwing *fire.* He had one of the most feared fastballs of all time.

Satchel had different names for his fastball. Sometimes he called it his "bee ball." Or "trouble ball." Or "jump ball." Or "Long Tom." Whatever its name, the batter knew one thing. He had to be really sharp to hit it!

Satchel joined the Pittsburgh Crawfords in 1932. The team was started by a black man named Gus Greenlee, who was involved in gambling. He wanted to build the best team in the history of black baseball. And he did. Five members of the Crawfords are now in the Baseball Hall of Fame.

Catcher Josh Gibson was almost as famous as Satchel. Josh was called the black Babe Ruth because he hit so many home runs. One season he hit eighty-nine—that was twenty-nine more than the Babe's record. But this record didn't count because Josh was not on a major-league team.

Josh Gibson's short, smooth swing rocketed the ball over fences everywhere. His most famous homer was in Yankee Stadium.

Another black team had rented the stadium for a game with the Crawfords. When it was his turn at bat, Josh hit the ball so hard and so far, it flew over the left-field stands. It went right out of the park. No other player—not Dave Winfield, not Mickey Mantle, not even Babe Ruth—has ever done that.

Judy Johnson was another famous teammate of Satchel's. He played third base for the Crawfords. Like all great players at the "hot corner," Judy was quick as a cat and had a rifle arm.

Oscar Charleston usually played first base for the Crawfords. But he was such a great all-around athlete that he could play any position. And sometimes that is just what he did. He'd play all nine positions in a single game!

Cool Papa Bell played outfield for the Crawfords. The fans loved him because he was such a bold base runner. He turned singles into doubles and doubles into triples or

Judy Johnson (above), Oscar
Charleston (above right), and
Cool Papa Bell played together
for the Pittsburgh Crawfords.

homers. Nobody could run as fast as Cool
Papa. Satchel often roomed with Cool Papa
Bell. He once said that Cool Papa could flip
off a light switch and be in bed before the
room was dark! That might be one of
Satchel's tall tales. But anyone who saw
Cool Papa knew he was the fastest runner
around.

Not only did Gus Greenlee put together a great team, he brought back the Negro National League. That was the league Rube Foster had started. In 1937 a second league was formed. The Negro American League. There were lots of good teams around, but the Crawfords were tops. And wherever they played, the star attraction was always Satchel.

Satchel had no change-up or curve ball. But he won game after game with his blazing fastball and his amazing confidence. Sometimes Satchel was so sure he would win, he would tell the batter exactly what kind of pitch he was going to throw. And still he'd strike the batter out. Other times he would order his outfield off the field!

In barnstorming games Satchel pitched against some of the greatest white major-league pitchers of the day. And he beat them. Satchel earned more money than most white players in the major leagues.

Here is Satchel Paige with Dizzy Dean, the best major-league pitcher of his time. Dizzy played against Satchel in barnstorming games and called him the greatest pitcher ever.

Still, he was a black man. And he had to live with prejudice. He would not play in any city where he and his teammates could not get a decent hotel and a decent meal.

He played on all-black baseball teams for almost forty years. That was some record.

Like Jackie Robinson, Satchel finally did get to the major leagues. And he set a record there, too. It's a record that will never be broken. Satchel became the oldest rookie in baseball history when the Cleveland Indians took him on in 1948.

The Cleveland Indians were in a tight race for the American League pennant that year. They needed another good pitcher. Satchel filled the bill. Satchel was either thirty-nine, forty-two, or forty-eight at the time. He had a 6–1 season, and the Cleveland Indians did go on to clinch the pennant *and* win the World Series.

Satchel only lasted two seasons with the Indians. But he kept on pitching until 1965.

Lots of people, including Satchel himself, thought Satchel should have been the very first black player on a major-league team. It didn't work out that way. But Satchel never had anything except great things to say about the man who was the first. Jackie Robinson.

5

Crossing the Color Line

In 1945, World War II was over. It was a war for freedom. It was a war in which thousands of black soldiers had given their lives. "If a black man is good enough to die for his country," many people were saying, "he's good enough to play baseball."

But was there a white baseball man with the guts to be the first to sign a black player? And was there a black player with the guts to be the first?

The answer to both questions was yes!

Branch Rickey was the president and

general manager of the Brooklyn Dodgers. He had been managing baseball teams nearly all his life. More than anything, he wanted the Dodgers to win the World Series.

The Dodgers were an old team. They needed new, young players. Branch Rickey knew there were some really good young black players in the Negro leagues. He was willing to sign some if it meant his team could win the Series.

Branch Rickey wanted to bring a black into major-league baseball for another reason too.

Many years ago he had been the coach of a college baseball team. The team had only one black player.

On a trip to Indiana the black player was told he couldn't stay in the hotel with the rest of the team. Branch Rickey finally got the hotel to let the man room with him. Later, when Branch went to the room, he found the man sitting on his bed. He was staring at his hands.

"Black skin!" he cried out. "Oh, if only it was white."

Branch Rickey saw how cruel it was to judge a man by the color of his skin. It was something he never forgot. But he knew he had to find a very special black player to cross the color line. And he wanted to keep the search quiet. So Branch Rickey announced that he was starting a new black team. The Brooklyn Brown Dodgers. This was just a trick. It let Branch send out his baseball scouts. They could look openly for the best players on the black teams. Not even the scouts knew the real reason why Branch was interested in the black players.

One of the scouts soon singled out a young shortstop on the Kansas City Monarchs.

Jackie Robinson is your man, the scout told Branch Rickey.

Jackie Robinson was born in 1919 and grew up in Pasadena, California. His family was poor. But Jackie was smart, and Jackie was great at sports. In college he was a star on the football team. And the track team. And the basketball team. And the baseball team.

In World War II, Jackie became an officer of an all-black unit in the army. He was one of the very first black officers.

He was a man who always stood up for his rights. When he was in the army, Jackie lived in Texas. At that time blacks had to sit in the back of city buses, in the worst seats. But on army buses blacks got to sit wherever they wanted. One time Jackie got on an army bus. The driver told him to get in back. But Jackie refused to do it. The bus driver had him arrested! Jackie went on trial, and he was found not guilty.

Jackie could have done what the bus driver said. But he was not that kind of person. He was willing to go through a lot for what was right. This was important to Branch Rickey.

Branch Rickey asked Jackie Robinson to come to Brooklyn to meet him. Jackie was not sure why Branch Rickey wanted to see him so badly. But he soon found out!

Branch told him flat out. He wanted Jackie Robinson for his team. The Brooklyn Dodgers. Not the Brooklyn Brown Dodgers.

Then Branch gave Jackie a taste of what he was going to hear from fans and players on other teams. For three hours he called Jackie every bad name. He described all kinds of mean situations. Then he told Jackie, "You cannot respond to any of this."

Jackie asked, "Do you want a ballplayer who's afraid to fight back?"

"I want a ballplayer with the guts *not* to fight back," Branch answered. "If you fight or answer the insults, you will lose. And so will all the other black players who are waiting to play. You must promise me that you will hold your temper and your tongue."

Jackie Robinson made that promise. On October 25, 1945, he signed a contract with Branch Rickey. It was big news on sports pages all across the country. In black newspapers it made front-page headlines.

Many people thought Branch Rickey made the wrong choice. Even players in the Negro leagues. Jackie Robinson was a rookie, people pointed out. He had played only one year with the Monarchs. Yes, he was a good hitter and a daring base runner. But out in the field he wasn't that great.

Branch knew all this. But he had a plan. Jackie would start out with the Montreal Royals. This was a farm team for the Dodgers. It was a place where young players like Jackie could get training for the major leagues.

The 1946 season was a good one for the Montreal Royals. And a good one for Jackie, too. He played well, and the fans liked him.

The next year Jackie was ready for the Dodgers. But right away there was trouble.

During spring training some Dodgers said they would sign a letter. The letter demanded that Jackie get off the team.

The manager of the team found out about the letter. He called all the players together. He told them that Jackie was staying. Anyone who didn't want to play with him could go to another team. That was the end of the letter. But there was more trouble.

Right at the start of the season, two

teams said they would not play against the Dodgers. They would go on strike. The teams were the Philadelphia Phillies and the St. Louis Cardinals. But the president of the league was tough. If the two teams wouldn't play, he promised to throw them out of the league for the rest of the season. That was the end of the strike. But that was still not the end of the trouble.

A few weeks later the Phillies arrived at Ebbets Field for their first game with the Dodgers. From the moment the game started, the Phillies called Jackie every name in the book.

Jackie could do nothing. He could say nothing. He'd made a promise to Branch Rickey. The other Dodgers knew this. And they felt bad for Jackie.

The next day the Dodgers told the Phillies and their manager to leave Jackie alone. Even the Dodgers who wanted to keep Jackie off the team stuck up for him now.

The games went on. There were more hard times ahead for Jackie. But he knew one thing. He really and truly was one of the Dodgers.

For ten seasons Jackie Robinson played second base for the Brooklyn Dodgers. He played in six World Series. He was voted Most Valuable Player in 1949. His lifetime batting average was .311. In 1962 he was elected to the Baseball Hall of Fame. It was another first. No black man had ever received this honor before.

But for millions of fans Jackie Robinson meant so much more than awards and averages. He was not just a hero for black people. He was a hero for the whole country.

6

A Place of Honor

Every year about 300,000 people visit the Baseball Hall of Fame in Cooperstown, New York. Fans read the names on the plaques. They read about the records these men set. For a baseball player there is no greater honor.

Until the 1970s no Negro league players were in the Hall of Fame. Hardly any were eligible, because they had never played on major-league teams. But whose fault was that, anyway?

When Ted Williams, the great Red Sox slugger, was voted into the Hall of Fame in

1966, he said, "I hope that someday Satchel Paige and Josh Gibson will be voted into the Hall of Fame as symbols of the great Negro players who are not here only because they weren't given a chance."

Ted Williams's wish came true.

In the late 1960s the rules were changed so that the superstars of the Negro leagues could get the honor they deserved. Satchel Paige was the first. He was elected to the Hall of Fame in 1971. Josh Gibson came next, along with Buck Leonard, in 1972. So far, out of more than 200 Hall of Famers, eleven are players who made their name in the Negro leagues.

At last, at long last, they are where they belong.

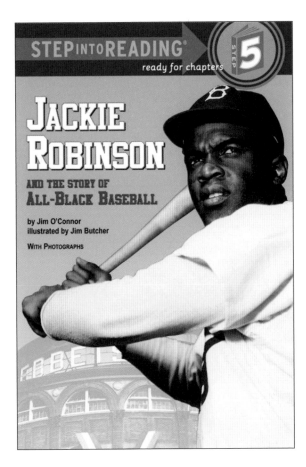

Teachers Guide

This guide meets the following common core standards:

INFORMATIONAL TEXT—KEY IDEAS AND DETAILS

2. Determine the main idea of a text and explain how it is supported by key details; summarize the text.
3. Explain events, procedures, ideas, or concepts in a historical, scientific, or technical text, including what happened and why, based on specific information in the text.

READING: LITERATURE

3. Describe in depth a character, setting, or event in a story or drama, drawing on specific details in the text (e.g., a character's thoughts, words, or actions).

READING: FOUNDATIONS

4. Use context to confirm or self-correct word recognition and understanding, rereading as necessary.

Pre-Reading Activity

Divide students into three groups and your room into three stations. At each station have a poster at each station. Have children move from each station and brainstorm together the answers to the following questions:

Station 1: What do you know, if anything, about Jackie Robinson?

Station 2: What is *discrimination*? List any examples you can think of?

Station 3: What is the history of Major League Baseball?

After each group has visited all three stations, discuss each poster before beginning to read the first chapter.

Comprehension

Being able to summarize a chapter is a key skill for comprehension. Explain to your students that a summary is the BIG IDEA in the chapter or the POINT. It's probably what they would tell a friend who forgot to do the reading/homework.

Chapter:	A two sentence summary of what happened:	Important details from the chapter:
1		
2		
3		
4		
5		
6		

Have students work together to find quotes from the text that explain the following facts and terms:

Important facts or terms:	A quote from the book that explains it:
April 15, 1947, was an important day in baseball history.	
In the 1940s, people were not treated equally.	
Some fans treated Jackie Robinson badly.	
Jackie earns his fans.	
The negro leagues lose popularity.	

Comprehension

Have students create a web about Jackie Robinson as they read the text. They should look for specific and important facts about his childhood, his influence on professional baseball, and evidence of his character and personality. Once webs are completed, have them compare the information collected in pairs and revise.